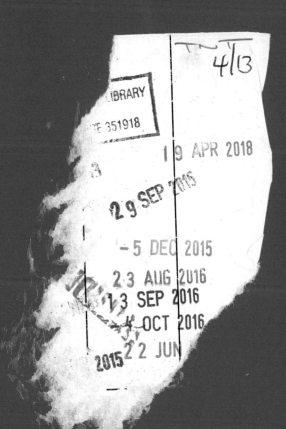

SCHOLASTIC discover more™

rainforest

By Penelope Arlon
and
Tory Gordon-Harris

Free digital book

From pygmy marmosets to giant gorillas, meet some of the most fun and fascinating animals on the planet.

monkeys!

Monkeys and apes of the rainforest

A digital companion to **Rainforest**

SCHOLASTIC dis

Download your all-new digital book,

Monkeys!

Log on to
www.scholastic.com/discovermore
Enter this special code:

RCDWKNPXN932

Go ape!

Chimpanzees are cute and clever, but are you?
Check out the questions and see how you do.

1 **Chimps use tools, like humans do. Which ones do they use?**

A Spades to dig up fruit
B Sticks to fish out insects
C Knives and forks to eat with

2 **What do chimps eat?**

A Bananas
B Honey
C Meat

3 **Chimps belong to which group?**

A Old world monkeys
B New world monkeys
C Great apes

4 **We know that chimps communicate – but how do they do it?**

A They use sign language.
B They touch one another and make faces.
C They use calls – sounds that have meanings.

Take fun monkey quizzes – are you as cute and clever as a monkey?

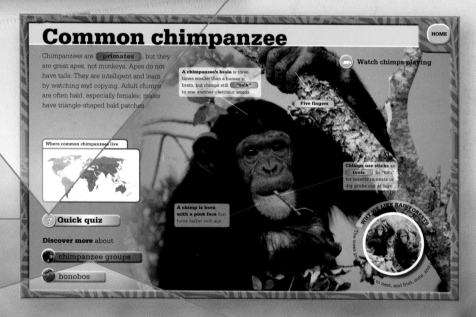

Common chimpanzee

HOME

Chimpanzees are primates, but they are great apes, not monkeys. Apes do not have tails. They are intelligent and learn by watching and copying. Adult chimps are often bald, especially females; males have triangle-shaped bald patches.

Watch chimps playing

A chimpanzee's brain is three times smaller than a human's brain, but chimps still **"talk"** to one another – without words.

Five fingers

Chimps use sticks as tools to "fish" for insects in nests or dig grubs out of logs.

Where common chimpanzees live

A chimp is born with a pink face that turns darker with age.

WHY WE LIKE RAINFORESTS

The trees provide... to nest, and fruit, nuts, and...

? Quick quiz

Discover more about

chimpanzee groups

bonobos

Read in-depth information about monkeys and great apes.

chimpanzee group

A chimpanzee lives in a group with other chimps of all ages. There may be more than 100 chimps living together, or as few as 15. There is a strong hierarchy, with a large male as the head. The top male is often chosen by females of the group, and he has to keep the support of the females to stay in control. Males may fight one another for power, but they work together to guard their territory (the area where they live), taking turns to patrol it. The chimps hunt together and share food. They use branches to make nests in trees, lining them with leaves and twigs.

COMMON CHIMP—FAST FACTS	
Scientific name	Pan troglodytes
Height	1.2–1.7 m (3–5 ft)
Weight (male)	40–60 kg (88–132 lbs)
Weight (female)	32–47 kg (70–104 lbs)

Chimpanzees sleep, rest, and feed high in trees. There are around 200,000 common chimpanzees left in the wild.

It's simple to get your digital book. Go to the website (see left), enter the code, and download the book. Make sure you open it using Adobe Reader.

Consultants: Dr George C. McGavin;
Kim Dennis-Bryan, PhD
Art Director: Bryn Walls
Designer: Ali Scrivens
Managing Editor: Miranda Smith
Cover Designer: Neal Cobourne
DTP: John Goldsmid
Digital Photography Editor: Stephen Chin
Visual Content Project Manager:
Diane Allford-Trotman
**Executive Director of Photography,
Scholastic:** Steve Diamond

Library of Congress Cataloging-in-Publication
Data Available

Distributed in the UK by
Scholastic UK Ltd
Westfield Road
Southam, Warwickshire
England CV47 0RA

ISBN 978 1 407 13657 8

10 9 8 7 6 5 4 3 2 1   13 14 15 16 17

Printed in Singapore   46
First published 2013

Contents

All about rainforests

Rainforest animals

All about rainforests

Welcome to our planet's oldest
and most spectacular land habitat.
Rainforests are thick with trees
that thrive in the hot and humid
climate. They are home to amazing
plants and animals, including
millions still to be discovered.

What is a rainforest?

Imagine walking through a thick, hot forest, across soft, damp ground, listening to buzzing insects, howling monkeys, and screeching birds. Welcome to the tropical rainforest.

NORTH AMERICA

scarlet macaw......

The rainforests of Central and South America also cover the islands of the Caribbean.

AFRICA

Gaboon viper

CENTRAL AMERICA

The Amazon rainforest is the world's largest.

EQUATOR

keel-billed toucan

Amazon R.

SOUTH AMERICA

There are always about 12 hours of daylight at the Equator – plenty of sunshine all year!

Where are they?

Tropical rainforests, sometimes also called jungles, are found near the Equator – the imaginary line that runs around the middle of the Earth. The Sun shines hottest at the Equator.

whitetoe tarantula

Only 6 percent of Earth's surface is rainforest, yet

Rainforest weather cycle Perfect weather for plants

1 Hot sun
The temperature in the rainforest can be 30°C (86°F). Plants absorb sunlight and turn it into energy to help them grow.

2 Heavy rain
Up to 4 m (13 ft) of rain falls each year. The plants draw water up through their roots to the tips of their leaves.

3 Many plants
Leaves give off water vapour, and mist rises to form clouds and more rain. Plants thrive in so much rain and sun.

tiger·····

ASIA

proboscis
monkey

The Southeast Asian rainforests reach from mainland Asia across hundreds of islands to the northern tip of Australia.

Congo R.

longhorn
beetle

Lush rainforests stretch across west central Africa, around the River Congo.

AUSTRALASIA

ring-tailed
lemur

Jungle in danger
People are cutting the rainforests down. This not only puts plants and animals in danger, but also affects the health of our whole planet. Find out more on pages 66–67.

flying fox

over half of all plant and animal species live there.

A rainbow of rainforest

Rainforest animals are very colourful. Colour can camouflage, attract other animals, or warn that something is poisonous. Sometimes it is to show off!

flatid leaf bug

red lory

red leaf beetle

Wallace's golden birdwing

strawberry poison dart frog

Brazilian rainbow boa

eighty-eight butterfly

scarab beetle

postman butterfly

blushing phantom butterfly

keel-billed toucan

scarlet macaw

Attacus atlas moth

yellow-banded poison dart frog

strawberry poison dart frog

clearwing moth

fruit-piercing moth

golden poison frog

eyelash viper

great hornbill

animals

festive Amazon parrot

tailed jay butterfly

Helena morpho butterfly

birdwing butterfly

blue poison dart frog

lorikeet

panther chameleon

red-legged honeycreeper

saberwing hummingbird

Palmer's tree frog

red-eyed tree frog

shining leaf chafer

longhorn beetle

chestnut-headed bee-eater

malachite butterfly

crimson-rumped toucanet

leaf mimic katydid

orchid bees

harlequin poison frog

emerald tree boa

blue-and-gold macaw

peafowl

green iguana

Madagascar giant day gecko

caterpillar

orange-barred sulphur butterfly

green weevil

Top to bottom

A rainforest is like a very tall building with different floors. Each floor, or layer, is home to certain plants and animals, some of which never visit the ground.

The emergent layer

In this windy layer, some trees burst through the roof. The branches at the top spread out, some to the size of two football fields, and fill with leaves to soak up sunlight.

...lantern fly

The canopy

The canopy is the hot roof of the rainforest. The tall trees spread out their branches and burst with leaves to absorb sunlight and bear fruit. They provide plenty of food, so most rainforest animals live here.

......blue morpho butterfly

.....cotton-top tamarin

The understorey

Very little of the sunlight that the rainforest receives reaches the damp, shady understorey. Plants here grow big leaves to catch whatever light they can. Snakes twist around the vines that climb the tree trunks, insects buzz, and tree frogs thrive in the dripping, steamy air.

lemur leaf frog

blunt-headed vine snake

The forest floor

Only 2 percent of sunlight reaches the hot forest floor. The ground is damp from all the rain. Insects scuttle around, and colourful fungi grow out of dead wood.

esmeralda butterfly

Stegolepis

cup fungus

13

The forest floor

The forest floor is a shadowy maze of tree trunks. Few new plants can find enough sunlight to grow. Dangerous predators creep up on prey among the trees.

The stinkhorn mushroom has a foul smell to attract flies to spread its spores.

Hairy hunters

Large tarantulas emerge from their silk-lined burrows after dark to hunt for insects and small reptiles and mammals.

tarantula

termite mound

termite

Fantastic fungi

Forest-floor fungi are very important recyclers. They break down dead plants, putting nutrients back into the soil.

Mini-recyclers

Insects such as beetles, ants, and termites clear away decaying wood, leaves, and dead animals that would otherwise pile up on the forest floor.

It can take ten minutes for a single raindrop to reach the

The cassowary's hard crest may help the bird push through thick plants to forage for food.

Mammoth mammals

Few plant-eating mammals live here, since most leaves grow higher up. But a few, like this rhinoceros, trample through and eat new growth.

The mushroom-shaped part of this fungus contains the spores that will grow into new fungi.

Big birds

The southern cassowary is a huge bird that can be found on the floors of Southeast Asian jungles.

Snakes

Snakes are always quietly present on the forest floor. The bite of a king cobra can kill an elephant.

floor from the canopy above.

The busy canopy

High up in the leafy canopy, fruits and flowers provide plenty of food for an abundant variety of wildlife.

Monkeys

Monkeys screech as they swing around the canopy. The spider monkey above, searching for food among the leaves, lives in a large troop.

Three-toed sloths

Slow-moving sloths hang upside down on branches.

Parrots screech among the treetops.

There is always danger in the canopy. Everything is looking for a meal.

emerald tree boa

doris butterfly

Quetzal
Hundreds of kinds of brightly coloured birds live in the canopy, eating fruit and insects that live there.

Green iguana
Huge reptiles lurk on tree branches. This green iguana can grow to be 2 m (6.5 ft) long.

Leaf beetle
The mass of leaves, flowers, and fruits provides constant food for insects, which in turn are food for predators.

Sloths visit the forest floor only to poo.

Hall of fame

The rainforest has more kinds of plants and animals than any other habitat does. So it's not surprising that some record breakers of the entire natural world live here.

BIGGEST FLOWER
The giant rafflesia flower can grow to 1 m (3 ft) in diameter. It smells like rotten meat!

STINKIEST FRUIT
The durian fruit smells like onions and smelly socks, but some people say it tastes delicious!

LOUDEST ANIMAL
The howler monkey of the Amazon can be heard from 30 km (19 miles) away.

BIGGEST LEAF
The leaves of the African raffia palm can grow up to 25 m (82 ft) long and 3 m (10 ft) wide, making them the biggest in the world.

The River Amazon in South America holds more

NIFTIEST SWINGER

Gibbons can cover over 9 m (30 ft) in one leap. Their long arms help them swing from branch to branch.

BIGGEST SNAKE

The green anaconda, the biggest snake in the world, can be more than 8.8 m (29 ft) long.

SLOWEST ANIMAL

Sloths move really slowly because they mainly eat leaves, which give them little energy.

FASTEST FLAPPER

Hummingbirds can flap their wings 80 times a second. They are the only birds that can fly backwards.

BIGGEST BUTTERFLY

The Queen Alexandra's birdwing butterfly is only slightly smaller than this open book!

BIGGEST SCALED FISH

At 3 m (10 ft) in length, the arapaima is the biggest scaled freshwater fish.

freshwater than any other river in the world does.

Fight for light

For a plant to grow in the rainforest, it has to work hard to compete for light. Plants have some sneaky ways of competing.

Bromeliads are almost always found in American rainforests.

Bowls of water

Some bromeliads grow on the forest floor, but most take root on high tree branches, where it's lighter. Their leaves may form bowls for holding water, some big enough for insects and even frogs to live in.

Buttress roots

Some trees grow roots, known as buttress roots, up their trunks for extra support and stability in the thin soil. The buttress roots enable them to grow even taller, towards the light.

buttress root

.....orchid

Treetop plants

The seeds of epiphytes, such as bromeliads, orchids, mosses, and lichens, grow on the sunlit surfaces of other plants without harming them. They get water and nutrients from dew, rainwater, plant debris, and moisture from the air.

Tree killers

Strangler fig seeds stick to the tops of trees. They then send roots down to the ground; these sprout branches and eventually squeeze the trees to death.

Liana vines

Lianas grow up trees, planting roots into the bark. When they reach the canopy, they send roots back down to the ground to secure themselves.

Tree cycle As one tree dies, the fight to take its place begins.

1 Fallen tree

When a tree falls down in the forest, it leaves a gap where light can enter.

2 New growth

Young saplings race to be the tree that replaces the dead one.

3 Relocation

If it's squashed, the stilt palm can grow new roots and move itself away.

Many trees produce leaves only at the sunlit canopy.

Amazing plants

In the rainforest, plants often have to be bigger or more cunning to survive and make baby plants. They often attract animals for help.

The flowers are the perfect length for a hummingbird's beak.

Finding help

A flower needs pollen to produce seeds. The heliconia attracts a hummingbird with its sweet nectar. Pollen rubs onto the bird, and the bird takes it to another heliconia flower.

Hummingbirds are among the few birds that can hover while flying.

Night flowers

The shaving brush tree is unusual – it opens its flowers only at night. It has a cheesy smell that attracts bats to sip its nectar and spread its pollen.

The leaves of some plants are so large that

Giant plants

The giant Amazon water lily has enormous leaves, to take up as much light as it can.

fly

Meat-eaters

The pitcher plant makes a delicious nectar that attracts insects into its deadly leaves. It then absorbs them.

Smelly flowers

The rafflesia smells like rotten meat, which flies love. The flies then spread the pollen from flower to flower.

shaving brush tree flower

Seed dispersal

Even fish help plants. The pacu of the River Amazon eats fallen fruit and spreads the seeds.

locals use **them as umbrellas in the rain.**

Rainforest animals

As you trek through the forest, you may see
a bright bird's feathers, a poisonous frog,
or an army of leaf-cutter ants. The rainforest is
home to about half the world's animal species.
Most primates (apes, monkeys, and lemurs),
such as these marmosets, live in jungles.

Central and South

Central and South America have the largest area of rainforest in the world, the vast majority of which is in the Amazon basin.

The jaguar's spotted coat blends perfectly into the understorey.

Amazon basin

AMAZON FACTS

RAINFOREST AREA
About 6.7 million sq. km (2.6 million sq. miles)

INDIGENOUS POPULATION
About 1 million native people

BIGGEST MAMMAL
Baird's tapir

TOP PREDATORS
Jaguar, harpy eagle, giant otter, boa

MOST ENDANGERED SPECIES
Ameerega ingeri – a type of poison dart frog. Only one has ever been found, in Colombia in 1970.

Jaguars
The stealthy jaguar is the top predator in the tropical American rainforests. It is not found anywhere else in the world.

American rainforests

toucan

Rainforest wildlife

Exotic birds

These jungles are rich with exotic birds. The tiny country of Panama has more bird species than all of North America does.

King swingers

South American monkeys, like this spider monkey, are the only ones that use their tails as an extra limb for gripping branches while swinging.

Rainforest people

Of the 400 tribes of rainforest people, most have been influenced by the outside world. A few, however, are still isolated.

Creepy-crawlies

Nobody knows how many insect species live in the rainforest, but each tree may hold several hundred different species.

15 percent of all bird species are found in the Amazon.

The River Amazon

Tropical rainforests often have giant rivers flowing through them because of all the rain. The mighty River Amazon weaves through the rainforest, with over 1,000 tributaries flowing into it.

This emergent tree has burst through the canopy.

Food source
Many tribes live near the Amazon and use it as a source of food and a way to travel.

Pink dolphins
The River Amazon has dolphins living in it. They are unusual because they turn pink as they get older!

canoe

The amazing Amazon

The Amazon carries more freshwater than any other river in the world. It is home to a tremendous amount of freshwater life, provides a source of drinking water to many land animals, and supports huge numbers of plants in and around it.

Danger! Watch out! The river is a dangerous place.

Caimans

The caiman – a type of alligator – lurks at the water's edge, ready to snap up thirsty animals.

Piranhas

With razor-sharp teeth, red-bellied piranhas are able to strip an animal to the bone.

Giant otters

The giant otter is the river's top predator. It eats fish, snakes, and even small caimans.

In some places, the river can be 10 km (6 miles) wide!

Amazon people

The Amazon rainforest is home to about 400 tribes of people, each with their own area, language, and culture.

Life in peril

There are about 32,000 Yanomami people living on the border between Brazil and Venezuela. Their land is now threatened by logging (cutting trees) and illegal gold mining.

Jungle city

Most people living in the rainforest live like the Yanomami, but there are a few cities in the rainforest, too. Iquitos is the largest city in the world that cannot be reached by road.

The Yanomami use about 500 kinds of plants for food, medicine, building and other useful products.

The Yanomami

Yanomami life The people live in harmony with the rainforest.

One big house

The Yanomami people live in groups of up to 400. A group lives in a single large house called a *shabono*.

Hunting food

The men hunt and fish. They use curare, a poison from plants, on the tips of their arrows.

Gardening

The Yanomami women tend to the 60 types of plants that they grow in their gardens.

may pierce their noses and ears.

Mini-creatures

Although you may not see them all unless you look very closely, the Amazon forest floor is home to millions of scuttling mini-creatures.

This tarantula is eating a bird.

Goliath bird-eating spiders

This tarantula is one of the biggest in the world. It would fill a dinner plate! It doesn't spin webs; instead, it hunts on the ground.

Azteca ants

Azteca ants live on cecropia trees. The trees provide the ants with a syrup to eat, and in return the ants defend the trees from predators.

Over 90 percent of all species in the Amazon are insects.

This crazy-coloured caterpillar will become a Borocera moth.

Scorpions

A scorpion has huge claws for grabbing prey, and a venomous stinger at the end of its tail to kill prey and for defence.

Caterpillars

The rainforest is filled with bright, hairy caterpillars, many of which are highly poisonous.

It is thought that the larvae, or young, eat wood, but they have never been seen.

. tarantula

Giant beetles

This titan longhorn beetle is the biggest beetle in the Amazon rainforest. Its sharp mandibles, or jaws, could cut a pencil in half or tear human flesh.

▶▶▶ **Find out more**
about poisonous animals on page 38.

and there are many yet to be found.

Mud-puddling butterflies

Male mud-puddling butterflies may transfer the

They drink what?

Pierid butterflies gather together in large groups to drink minerals from the mud. This is known as mud puddling. Mineral salts are hard to find in the rainforest, but animal urine and blood mix into the mud and provide a good source.

mineral salts to female butterflies.

Who eats who?

Every moment, something in the rainforest is eating something else. Who eats who sometimes runs in a line called a food chain.

A canopy food chain This chain starts in the air.

Eagle
The harpy eagle is a top predator, an animal that is never preyed on. It preys on monkeys.

Monkey
The capuchin monkey is an omnivore. It eats plants and animals, such as the mantis.

Mantis
The mantis is a carnivore. It waits patiently for insects to pass, then pounces.

Moth
The Atlas moth lives for only one to two weeks, and is at the bottom of this food chain.

Caimans are not top predators, because jaguars hunt them.

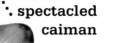
spectacled caiman

Caiman
This alligator is a carnivore. It catches fish in its teeth. It also snaps up mammals, such as deer, as they drink at the river.

Some animals are tricky to eat. Turn the page to see.

Using poison
This forest pit viper preys on small animals. It hangs from a tree. When prey such as this rat passes by, it strikes at lightning speed. It sinks its fangs into the rat, injecting venom to kill it. It swallows the rat whole.

Defence

Animals don't just let themselves be eaten — they go out of their way not to become lunch.

strawberry poison dart frog

Poison

Some animals use their bright colours to advertize that they are highly poisonous and taste disgusting, like these frogs.

Poison dart frogs are among the most poisonous creatures in the world.

Body armour

An armadillo has a hard, bony shell. It can roll into a ball to shield its soft underparts from attack.

armadillo

Spiky defence

Some trees grow vicious spines and thorns to protect themselves from hungry herbivores. It wouldn't be a good idea to climb this kapok tree.

The leaves of the gympie gympie tree in Asia are

Treetop escape

This white-faced capuchin monkey can swing quickly from branch to branch to make a speedy getaway.

Powerful sting

Bullet ants live in large colonies and protect their nests from predators by delivering powerful, poisonous stings. Their stings are said to be more painful than any other animal's.

Camouflage Can you see me?

When it is startled, an armadillo can jump up to 1.2 m (4 ft) into the air!

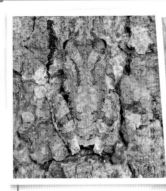

Not many hungry predators would spot this frog.

This bird dozes safely on a branch, looking like the branch itself!

Look very carefully, and you will spot a camouflaged spider.

poisonous – touch one and the pain can last two months!

Geckos have no eyelids. To keep their eyes clean, they

Cunning camouflage

The skin of this amazing mossy leaf-tailed gecko perfectly matches the bark of the tree that it is lying on. It can hide by changing the colour of its skin to blend in with any tree it chooses. It sleeps during the day, safe in the knowledge that it is hidden from hungry predators.

lick them! This gecko is probably asleep on the branch.

African rainforests

Most of the the rainforest area in Africa lies in the Congo basin on the Atlantic side of the continent. It is famous for its great apes.

...Congo basin

RAINFOREST FACTS

RAINFOREST AREA
1.875 million sq. km
(720,000 sq. miles)

INDIGENOUS POPULATION
500,000 native people

BIGGEST MAMMAL
African forest elephant

TOP PREDATORS
Leopard, crocodile, African rock python

MOST ENDANGERED SPECIES
Mountain gorilla – there are less than 790 known to be left in the wild.

Bugs

The African rainforest has some pretty strange creatures, as well as record breakers like this Goliath beetle – the heaviest beetle in the world, at up to 100 g (3.5 oz).

Among the biggest threats to large African rainforest

African rainforest wildlife

Great apes

The African rainforest is the only place in the world that is home to giant gorillas and clever chimpanzees (left).

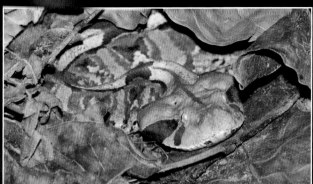

Deadly snakes

Hidden in the African rainforest lie some of the deadliest snakes on Earth, like this lethal Gaboon viper.

Odd mammals

The okapi is a stange animal with a long neck and a stripy bottom. It also has a 35-cm (14-inch) long blue tongue.

Birds

The rainforest has many exotic birds, including the African grey parrot, a brilliant mimic. It can copy almost any animal call.

wildlife are hunters who kill the animals for meat.

Forest people

There are many tribes in the African rainforest. The Efe are a tribe of hunter-gatherers who have lived in the forest for thousands of years.

Short stature

The African rainforest people are unusually short. They rarely grow taller than 1.5 m (5 ft).

Houses in the jungle

The Efe are constantly moving around the forest. They build temporary houses wherever they go.

The simple shelters are made out of branches and leaves.

The people believe that the forest protects them,

Honey collectors are highly regarded because taking honey makes bees very angry!

Efe diet

The Efe do not farm food. They hunt animals, eat plants, and gather foods such as honey

Food swap

The Efe trade their meat and honey for cloth and other products from people who live outside the forest.

Finding water

The Efe know every water supply in the jungle, including how to use liana vines to get it.

so they sing to make the forest happy.

Jungle swingers

One thing you are guaranteed to hear in any jungle is the chatter of the primates (monkeys and apes). Some live in large troops.

Spider monkeys live in troops of up to 35 and use lots of noises, such as barks and screams, to communicate.

The pygmy marmoset is the smallest primate in the world.

It's easy to recognize this monkey, because of its huge, bulgy nose!

Colobus monkeys are very agile. Unlike other monkeys, they have no thumbs.

Pygmy marmoset
HABITAT:
Amazon rainforest
MONKEY OR APE:
Monkey
LENGTH:
15 cm (6 ins)
DIET:
Tree gum, insects, spiders

Spider monkey
HABITAT:
Amazon rainforest
MONKEY OR APE:
Monkey
LENGTH:
66 cm (26 ins)
DIET:
Fruit, seeds, birds' eggs, spiders' eggs

Proboscis monkey
HABITAT:
Borneo
MONKEY OR APE:
Monkey
LENGTH:
75 cm (30 ins)
DIET:
Fruit, seeds, leaves

Colobus monkey
HABITAT:
West African rainforests
MONKEY OR APE:
Monkey
LENGTH:
75 cm (30 ins)
DIET:
Leaves, fruit, blossom

Chimps, gorillas, and orang-utans are great apes.

The male mandrill has a colourful nose and a blue bottom! It is the world's biggest monkey.

Chimps use tools, just like humans do. They use sticks and grass stems to fish for insects.

The gorilla is the biggest primate in the world.

Orang-utans build nests in trees to sleep in.

Mandrill

HABITAT:
West African rainforests
MONKEY OR APE:
Monkey
LENGTH:
81 cm (32 ins)
DIET:
Plants, small animals

Chimpanzee

HABITAT:
West and central Africa
MONKEY OR APE:
Ape
LENGTH:
160 cm (63 ins)
DIET:
Fruit, seeds, red colobus monkeys (they hunt them in troops)

Orang-utan

HABITAT:
Borneo and Sumatra
MONKEY OR APE:
Ape
LENGTH:
175 cm (69 ins)
DIET:
Fruit, insects, bird eggs, honey

Gorilla

HABITAT:
West and central Africa
MONKEY OR APE:
Ape
LENGTH:
180 cm (71 ins)
DIET:
Leaves, shoots, stems, fruit

Gibbons are lesser apes. Monkeys have tails; apes don't.

Madagascar

The African rainforest island of Madagascar is home to many animals that are endemic to the island – they are not found anywhere else in the world.

About as long as a man's arm, the Parson's chameleon is one of the largest chameleons.

······ **Madagascar**

RAINFOREST FACTS

RAINFOREST AREA
Madagascar is 587,041 sq. km (226,658 sq. miles). Once covered in rainforest, now only 10 percent remains.

POPULATION
22 million people on the island; about 20 ethnic groups

BIGGEST MAMMAL
Bushpig

TOP PREDATOR
Fossa

MOST ENDANGERED SPECIES
Madagascan pochard diving duck – there are only 60 left in the world.

Chameleons
Over half of all chameleon species live in Madagascar. They have tongues as long as their bodies and can change colour depending on their moods.

Giant elephant birds, standing 3 m (10 ft) tall, once

Island wildlife Unique creatures

Birds
Over half of the bird species found in Madagascar, like this sickle-billed vanga, are found exclusively here.

Mammals
The mammals in this rainforest are small. The catlike fossa is the biggest predator – about the size of a dog.

Insects
The rainforest is packed with insects. The hissing cockroach is a nocturnal carnivore that bears live young!

Lemurs
Lemurs are primates that live only in Madagascar. Many live in troops and leap through trees and across ground.

Parson's chameleon

49

Record-breaking web

The web

This web was made by a Darwin's bark spider, found in Madagascar. These spiders' webs can be as long as two school buses! They are the largest known webs in the world.

Amazing fact: a spiderweb

Darwin's
bark spider.

is the strongest known natural material on Earth.

Weird and wonderful

The rainforest is filled with many strange-looking creatures. Some are transparent, some are odd shapes, and some even glow!

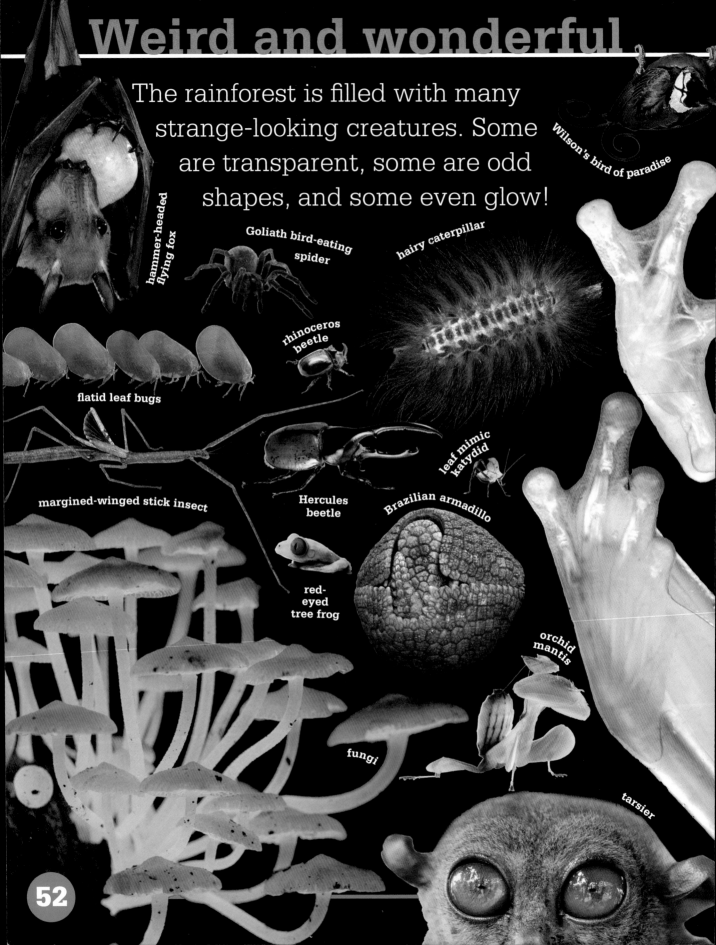

Wilson's bird of paradise

hammer-headed flying fox

Goliath bird-eating spider

hairy caterpillar

rhinoceros beetle

flatid leaf bugs

leaf mimic katydid

margined-winged stick insect

Hercules beetle

Brazilian armadillo

red-eyed tree frog

orchid mantis

fungi

tarsier

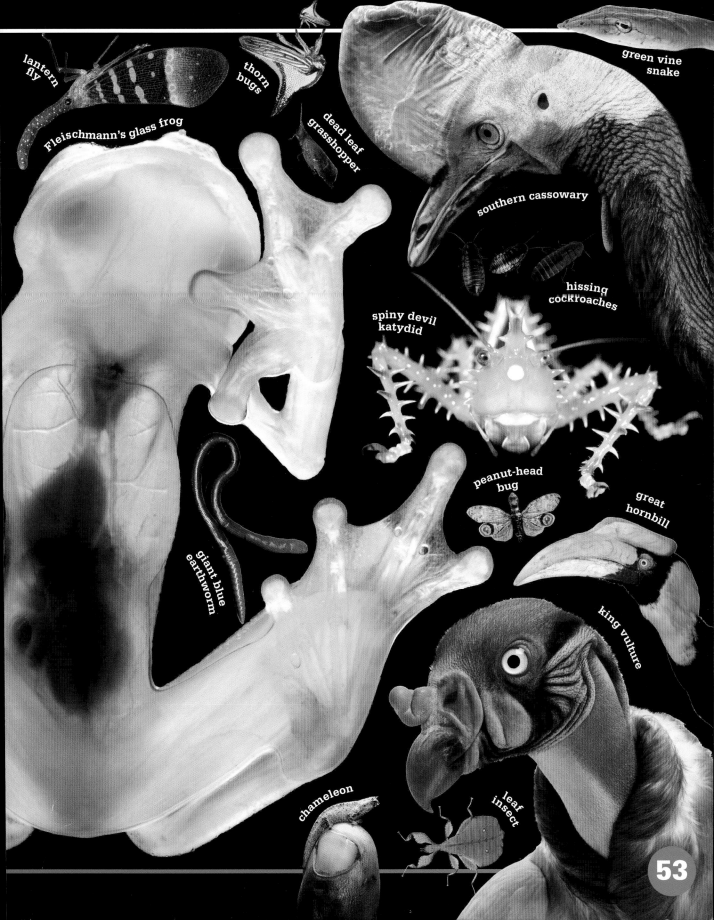

lantern fly

thorn bugs

green vine snake

Fleischmann's glass frog

dead leaf grasshopper

southern cassowary

hissing cockroaches

spiny devil katydid

peanut-head bug

great hornbill

giant blue earthworm

king vulture

chameleon

leaf insect

Asian rainforests

The Asian rainforests are among the oldest on Earth. They stretch from India all the way down to northern Australia, covering hundreds of islands in between.

People use these elephants for transport.

Papua New Guinea

RAINFOREST FACTS

COUNTRIES
India, Sri Lanka, Bhutan, Bangladesh, Burma, Thailand, Laos, Vietnam, Cambodia, Malaysia, Papua New Guinea, the Philippines, Indonesia, Australia

INDIGENOUS POPULATION
Hundreds of tribes in Papua New Guinea alone

BIGGEST MAMMAL
Asian elephant

TOP PREDATORS
Tiger, Burmese python, black eagle

MOST ENDANGERED SPECIES
Javan rhinoceros – there may be fewer than 45 left in the wild.

The orang-utan is the biggest primate of the Asian

Wildlife in the island forests

Atlas moths
The biggest moth in the world lives in the Southeast Asian rainforest. It is 30 cm (1 ft) wide.

Big cats
The Asian rainforests are home to the most famous big cat of all – the tiger. Its body can be 1.8 m (6 ft) long.

Tall trees
In the tall trees, animals have adapted to life in the air. This ornate tree snake can glide by thrusting out its body and flaring its ribs.

Elephants
The Asian elephant is smaller than African elephants and has smaller ears. It tramps through the forest, eating leafy plants and tree bark.

Australian forests
The northern Australian rainforests are not as rich in species as others are, but they do have tree kangaroos!

forests. It is found on the islands of Borneo and Sumatra.

After dark

As darkness falls in the Asian rainforests, strange creatures emerge. The hunters are awake, and their prey are in danger!

During the day, bats hang upside down in caves or trees. At night, millions fly off to find food.

Tigers live and hunt on their own.

Flying frogs

Wallace's flying frog hunts at night. When it spots prey on another tree, it glides to it.

Tapirs

The Malayan tapir snuffles around at night. It doesn't have good eyesight, but it has a great sense of smell, and big ears to listen for danger.

Stealthy tigers

In the pitch-black forest, the tiger is as quiet as a mouse and almost invisible as it stalks its prey. Once it is close enough, it pounces!

Flying foxes are the biggest bats in the world.

Giant bats

The flying fox uses its sharp eyesight and sense of smell to find food in the dark.

Female fireflies

These beetles have lights in their abdomens that they flash at night to attract mates.

..... flying fox

Huge eyes

A tarsier's eyeballs are enormous, which helps it see in the dark. It catches prey by jumping on it.

The Philippine tarsier has long fingers with fingernails. Two fingers on its back legs have claws for grooming.

Their wingspans can be up to 1.5 m (5 ft).

Papua New Guinea

Papua New Guinea, in the Pacific Ocean, is the only country in the world where the majority of the population lives in the rainforest.

Bird of paradise

Each tribe has its own style of dress. Tribes often use feathers from the bird of paradise.

Festival time

Many tribes come to the Mount Hagen Cultural Show to participate in the "sing-sing". They decorate themselves and perform for one another.

Huli tribe headdress

More than

Cutting trees

The Korowai tribe builds tree houses above the canopy. People cut trees and collect branches.

Building houses

This tree house is built on stilts 25 m (82 ft) above the ground. The whole tribe helps.

A safe home

The Korowai build these amazing houses to protect themselves from attacks by other tribes.

Asaro mudmen

These masks and body paints are made of mud.

Find out more ◀◀◀ about people of the rainforest on pages 30–31.

700 languages may be spoken in Papua New Guinea.

The essential rainforest

Humans are destroying Earth's most vital habitat. Tropical rainforests once covered 14 percent of the planet's land surface. Today they cover only about 6 percent, and many species of animals and plants, such as this pitcher plant, are endangered or extinct. What can you do to help protect the forests that remain?

Why rainforests matter

Rainforests are very important – not just to the plants, animals, and people who live there, but to every single person on Earth. If the rainforests disappeared, our lives would change.

Rainforest home

Most of the planet's biodiversity lives in rainforests. They are home to well over half of all animal and plant species.

leaf mimic katydid

Rainforests affect everyone

Help us breathe

Rainforest plants produce much of the oxygen that we breathe in so that we can live.

Clean our air

The plants absorb huge amounts of damaging carbon dioxide gas, which our cars create.

Produce rain

Rainforests produce a lot of the world's water, which travels to every country and falls as rain.

Turn to pages 66–67 to find out how our

macaw

Here are some of the ways that rainforests help us.

Keep us well
About 25 percent of all medicines that we use to stay healthy originate from rainforest plants.

Give us rubber
Did you know that rubber comes from the sap of rainforest trees? No rainforest, no wellies!

Feed us
Lots of the foods that we eat every day, such as tropical fruits, grow in the rainforest.

rainforests are in danger of disappearing forever.

How chocolate is made

All chocolate comes from the rainforest.

The Central American Aztecs used cacao beans as money!

1   Cacao tree
Chocolate is made from the pods, or fruits, of the cacao tree. The tree must grow in the shade – the understorey is perfect.

4 Packing the beans
Only when the beans are completely dry can they leave the rainforest. The dried beans are packed in sacks and sent to factories.

5 Melting the nibs
The beans are roasted, then rolled to remove the outer crusts. When the nib, or centre, of a bean is heated, it melts into a cocoa mass.

Only tiny jungle midges help cacao trees pollinate, so

2 Seeds

The pods are the size of footballs. There are about 30 beans, or seeds, inside each pod, surrounded by a moist pulp.

cacao beans

3 Heating and drying

The beans are picked and left in a pile for about 5–6 days, where they ferment. They are then laid out to dry. After 3–7 days, they turn brown.

6 Making the chocolate

Sugar and milk fats are added to the cocoa mass. The chocolate is swirled in machines to make it smooth. It is dried in moulds, then wrapped in packaging.

7 Ancient chocolate

Over 2,000 years ago, the Maya of Central America made and drank chocolate, mixing it with water, honey, or chillies!

it is hard to grow cacao anywhere but in rainforests.

Jungle in danger

In the time it takes you to read this book, an area of rainforest the size of two football fields will have been destroyed. The future of the rainforests is in jeopardy.

Deforestation

The loss of forest is called deforestation. Rainforests are cleared for wood and palm oil, to make room for farming, and by companies that mine for jewels and metals, like the aluminium used in drink cans.

Who suffers?

1 Local people

Many rainforest tribes are being forced away from their homes in the forest.

When trees are cut down for wood, the heavy machines churn up the soil and destroy the undergrowth, and plants can't regrow.

Some people think that by the year 2060,

The destruction of the rainforest affects us all.

2 Animals

Potentially 35 species of animal are becoming extinct every day.

3 Plants

Many plants, such as some orchid species, are disappearing forever.

4 Everyone

The foods, medicines, and other rainforest products that we use are being lost.

Global warming

Deforestation has been linked to global warming – the heating of the Earth. Carbon dioxide (CO_2) traps the Sun's heat and light and warms the air. Trees absorb CO_2 and help keep temperatures steady. If too many trees are cut down, Earth will heat up, and many plants and animals will die.

there will be no rainforests left.

Saving the rainforests

A few centuries ago, there was twice as much rainforest on Earth as there is today. Some governments and organizations are trying to help stop the destruction – you can, too.

Sustainability

Rainforest crops can be grown without clearing large areas of forest. These products are considered sustainable.

National parks

Some countries are turning huge areas of rainforest into parks that are protected by law. Tourists pay to visit and see amazing animals, such as orang-utans.

Mountain gorillas are now protected in Virunga National Park, Africa.

Rainforest food products can be gathered without

What can you do?

1 Learn

Find organizations that help save rainforests, and spread the word.

2 Recycle

Recycle paper, and tell others to, so that fewer trees need to be cut.

3 Be aware

Make sure that flowers and foods you buy are from sustainable sources.

▶▶ **Find out more** about endangered animals on pages 70–71.

Reforestation

Logging companies can replace cut trees by planting new ones. Replanting is called reforestation.

Zoos and parks

Many zoos and parks breed and study endangered rainforest animals, some of which are released back into the wild.

clearing huge **areas of rainforest.**

Last chance to see

Rainforests are disappearing fast, and all of the animals that live there are under threat. These animals are in danger of becoming extinct very soon.

rhinoceros hornbill

Queen Alexandra's birdwing butterfly

Madagascar serpent eagle

imperial parrot

Philippine eagle

tapir

hyacinth macaw

Bali starling

manatee

golden dragon fish

great green macaw

giant otter

red-headed vulture

black-handed spider monkey

white-cheeked gibbons

gorilla

Spix's macaw

yellow-crested cockatoo

poison dart frog

rufous hornbill

glasswing butterfly

red-crowned Amazon parrot

golden mantella frog

black-and-white ruffed lemur

chimpanzee

treehopper

katydid

postman butterfly

golden-headed lion tamarin

Sumatran tiger

electric blue gecko

Jungle survival

Plants sting you, animals may try to eat you, you get very wet, and you have to find food and water. Could you survive in the rainforest?

Sharpened bamboo makes a good spear for fishing.

Use campfire smoke at dawn and dusk to help repel insects.

Always shake out your boots and clothes before you put them on – spiders or scorpions might be hiding inside!

If you get lost, follow a river. Chances are good that you will eventually find people or even a town.

Watch what monkeys eat. Whatever they eat, you will be

Lots of water drips off leaves. If you angle the end of a leaf into a bottle, you can catch the water.

Cut open a liana vine and you might find freshwater inside it.

If you run out of food, try frying a handful of ants – they are rich in protein.

Never drink water straight from a river. Always boil it first, to get rid of any impurities.

Rub mud on your exposed skin. When it dries, it will form a crusty barrier against mosquitoes.

able to eat, too.

Interview with a

Name: Charith Senanayake
Profession: Managing director, Rainforest Rescue International, Sri Lanka

Q What do you do?

A I run Rainforest Rescue International, which works to educate people about the rainforest and to protect the little that remains.

Q How much of Sri Lanka's rainforest has been lost?

A Only 5 percent of the rainforest on the island exists today. Most has been cleared for timber and for farming crops like tea and rubber, which are exported to other countries.

The hump-nosed lizard is a "near threatened" species – its numbers are declining.

Q How does your organization help?

A We visit villages and schools to set up projects and educate people.

Q What sort of projects?

A Recently I asked a group of children to design a poster. They took photos in the rainforest, wrote text, then we printed it.

Q Do you help animals?

A Yes. At the moment we are building frog roads! We are making ponds that connect different parts of the rainforest, to encourage frogs to migrate from one area to another.

conservationist

Q Do you plant new trees?

A We study canopy trees and try to plant new ones in the hope that the rainforest will grow naturally around them. It is not always about replanting, however – it's about living in harmony with what remains. People need to use the rainforest, but they can use it in sensible ways.

Q What is your favourite rainforest animal?

A Definitely the slender loris, a wonderful little primate with enormous eyes that hunts insects at night. Unfortunately, it is an endangered species.

Q Do you have a least favourite rainforest animal?

A The leech. It's a very unpleasant bloodsucking worm that always seems to find bare skin to attach itself to!

Q Why is it important to save the rainforest?

A The rainforest is only one of the ecosystems in Sri Lanka, but it supports the others around it. If it disappeared, the wildlife in the rainforest would suffer and other life around it would, too.

Q What can we do to help?

A The best way to help save rainforests is to be aware. Try to make sure wood is from a sustainable source – that means the rainforest has not been harmed while cutting trees down. It's also good to recycle.

slender loris

leech

Glossary

ape
A large primate with no tail. Gorillas and chimpanzees are apes.

biodiversity
The range of different animals and plants living in a habitat.

camouflage
Natural colouring that helps animals blend in with their surroundings.

canopy
The layer of rainforest between the understorey and the emergent layer. Most rainforest animals live here.

carbon dioxide
A gas in the air that plants use to make food. All animals breathe out carbon dioxide. Carbon dioxide contributes to global warming.

colony
A large group of the same kind of animal living together.

conservationist
Someone who studies or practises the protection of natural areas, such as rainforests.

deforestation
The act of cutting down trees and vegetation to make room for farming or mining or to use the wood.

emergent layer
The highest layer of the rainforest, made up of the tops of the tallest trees. Birds and monkeys often live here.

epiphyte
A type of plant that usually grows on another plant and draws water and food from the air. Bromeliads and orchids are epiphytes.

extinct
No longer in existence, having died out.

ferment

To turn grain or fruit into alcohol, often by heat. Making chocolate involves fermentation.

food chain

A series of living things that depend on one another for food. A typical food chain starts when a plant is eaten by an animal. The plant-eating animal is then eaten by a meat-eating animal.

forest floor

The lowest layer of the rainforest, on the ground, where there is very little sunlight. Insects and fungi live here.

global warming

The warming of Earth's atmosphere, caused by increased carbon dioxide.

habitat

The place where an animal or plant usually lives or grows.

hunter-gatherer

Someone who hunts animals and gathers fruits and grains from the wild to eat.

monkey

A small primate with a tail. Mandrills and marmosets are monkeys.

predator

An animal or plant that eats other animals.

prey

An animal that is hunted and eaten by another animal or plant.

recycle

To change waste into new, reusable material.

spore

A seedlike cell that fungi and certain plants use to reproduce.

sustainability

The practice of making sure that rainforests are not totally destroyed, by reforestation and other methods of conservation.

understorey

The layer of rainforest between the forest floor and the canopy. It is damp, shady, and full of frogs, insects, and snakes.

The emerald tree boa lives in the rainforests of South America.

Index

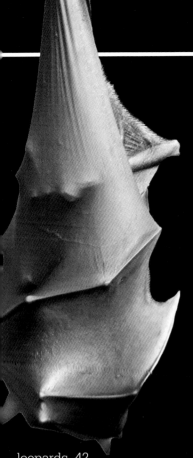

The flying fox hangs upside down to sleep, covering itself with its wings.

Thank you

Photography

1: Thomas Marent; 2–3: Media Bakery; 3tr, 4–5 (background), 4tl: Thomas Marent; 4tr: Wave Royalty Free/Alamy; 5tc: iStockphoto/Thinkstock; 6–7: Photodisc/Getty Images; 8tl: Lim Yong Hian/Shutterstock; 8l: Cezary Wojtkowski/age fotostock; 8–9 (background): iStockphoto/Thinkstock; 8 (scarlet macaws): Media Bakery; 8 (keel-billed toucan): Hemera/Thinkstock; 8 (whitetoe tarantula): Péter Gudella/Shutterstock; 8–9 (Gaboon viper): Eric Isselée/Shutterstock; 9tl: Vaara/iStockphoto; 9tc: Ola Dusegård/iStockphoto; 9tr: TommL/iStockphoto; 9 (tiger): JinYoung Lee/Shutterstock; 9 (proboscis monkey): iStockphoto/Thinkstock; 9 (longhorn beetle): Shariff Che'Lah/Fotolia; 9 (ring-tailed lemur): iStockphoto/Thinkstock; 9 (logs): Rouzes/iStockphoto; 9 (flying fox): Dean Bertoncelj/Dreamstime; 10 (flatid leaf bug): Thomas Marent; 10 (red lory): Jordan Tan/Dreamstime; 10 (red leaf beetle): Thomas Marent; 10 (Wallace's golden birdwing): Jens Stolt/Dreamstime; 10 (Brazilian rainbow boa): vitti_80/Fotolia; 10 (strawberry poison dart frog t): Dirk Ercken/Dreamstime; 10 (Attacus atlas moth): maggieddd/iStockphoto; 10 (eighty-eight butterfly): Ian Klein/Dreamstime; 10 (scarab beetle): Morley Read/iStockphoto; 10 (postman butterfly): Aleisha Knight/iStockphoto; 10 (scarlet macaw): Dirk Freder/iStockphoto; 10 (blushing phantom butterfly): Wikimedia Commons; 10 (strawberry poison dart frog b): iStockphoto/Thinkstock; 10 (clearwing moth): Dr. Morley Read/Shutterstock; 10 (yellow-banded poison dart frog): Ryszard Laskowski/Dreamstime; 10 (keel-billed toucan): Edurivero/Dreamstime; 10 (eyelash viper): iStockphoto/Thinkstock; 10 (fruit-piercing moth): Pan Xunbin/Shutterstock; 10 (golden poison frog): iStockphoto/Thinkstock; 10 (great hornbill): Awei/Shutterstock; 10 (orange-barred sulphur butterfly): Didier Descouens/Wikimedia Commons; 11 (festive Amazon parrot): Farinoza/Fotolia; 11 (tailed jay butterfly): Ivan Mikhaylov/iStockphoto; 11 (Helena morpho butterfly): Kiankhoon/Dreamstime; 11 (birdwing butterfly): Oliver Lenz/Fotolia; 11 (blue poison dart frog, rainbow lorikeet): iStockphoto/Thinkstock; 11 (red-legged honeycreeper): Steven Blandin/Dreamstime; 11 (Palmer's tree frog): Dr. Morley Read/Shutterstock; 11 (saberwing hummingbird): Steffen Foerster/iStockphoto; 11 (panther chameleon): Amwu/Dreamstime; 11 (shining leaf chafer, red-eyed tree frog, malachite butterfly, longhorn beetle, leaf mimic katydid): iStockphoto/Thinkstock; 11 (emerald tree boa): Hemera/Thinkstock; 11 (crimson-rumped toucanet): Steve Herrmann/Dreamstime; 11 (chestnut-headed bee-eater): Cowboy54/Dreamstime; 11 (orchid bees): Alan Wellings/Dreamstime; 11 (harlequin poison frog): Dr. Morley Read/Shutterstock; 11 (green iguana): iFocus/Shutterstock; 11 (blue-and-gold macaw): Andrew Burgess/Shutterstock; 11 (Madagascar giant day gecko): larus/Shutterstock; 11 (green weevil, caterpillar): iStockphoto/Thinkstock; 11 (peafowl): srijanroyc/Fotolia; 12–13 (background): Thomas Marent; 12–13 (vine): Sander Kamp/iStockphoto; 12 (emergent layer, lantern fly, cotton-top tamarin): Thomas Marent; 12 (blue morpho butterfly): PhotoTalk/iStockphoto; 12 (lemur leaf frog), 13 (blunt-headed vine snake, esmeralda butterfly, Stegolepis, cup fungus): Thomas Marent; 14 (background): zstockphotos/iStockphoto; 14l: Thomas Marent; 14tr: Alexander Podshivalov/Dreamstime; 14cr: Dinodia Photos/Alamy; 14br: VincentEOS/iStockphoto; 15 (background): iStockphoto/Thinkstock; 15l: Andy Gehrig/iStockphoto; 15tc: louise murray/Alamy; 15tr, 15bc: Thomas Marent; 15br: Omar Ariff Kamarul Ariffin/Dreamstime; 16–17 (background): Ricardo Sánchez/Wikimedia Commons; 16–17 (leaves): Lim Yong Hian/Shutterstock; 16cl: Thomas Marent; 16tr: Media Bakery; 16cr: Sas Cuyvers/Wikimedia Commons; 16b: vilainecrevette/iStockphoto; 17t: fivespots/Shutterstock; 17cr: Spiderstock/iStockphoto; 17bl: Thomas Marent; 17bc: Stockbyte/Thinkstock; 17br: Thomas Marent; 18–19 (background): Nataliia Natykach/Shutterstock; 18–19 (frames): Iakov Filimonov/Shutterstock; 18–19 (medals): DNY59/iStockphoto; 18tr: Henrik Hansson Globaljuggler/Wikimedia Commons; 18cl: Sutprattana/Dreamstime; 18bl: Joanne-Weston/iStockphoto; 18bc: David Liebman; 18–19b: Wouter Tolenaars/Dreamstime; 19tl: Lin Joe Yin/Dreamstime; 19tr: Jupiterimages/Thinkstock; 19cm: Tom Brakefield/Media Bakery; 19cr: wcpmedia/Shutterstock; 19br: Superbass/Wikimedia Commons; 20l: Pablo J Yoder/iStockphoto; 20r: Flavio Vallenari/iStockphoto; 21tl: Kyprianos Elisseou/iStockphoto; 21tr: Dr. Morley Read/Photo Researchers, Inc.; 21cl: Thomas Marent; 21bl: Vaara/iStockphoto; 21bc: Rob Broek/iStockphoto; 21br: Morley Read/Alamy; 22l: Anthony Mercieca/Photo Researchers, Inc.; 22–23 (background), 22–23b: Thomas Marent; 23tl: Chao-Yang Chan/Alamy; 23 (fly), 23tc: iStockphoto/Thinkstock; 23tr: Hemera/Thinkstock; 23br: Mark Smith/Photo Researchers, Inc.; 24–25, 26–27: Thomas Marent; 26tl: Planetary Visions Ltd.; 27tr: iStockphoto/Thinkstock; 27tl: Hemera/Thinkstock; 27ct: Thomas Marent; 27cb: Robertobra/Wikimedia Commons; 27bl: Gary L. Brewer/Shutterstock; 27br: iStockphoto/Thinkstock; 28–29, 28br: g01xm/iStockphoto; 28cl: NHPA/SuperStock; 29tl: Phototreat/iStockphoto; 29bl: cynoclub/iStockphoto; 29bc: Tatiana Volgutova/Dreamstime; 29br: Kevin Schafer/Media Bakery; 30tr: Jake Lyell/Alamy; 30bl: Wave Royalty Free/Alamy; 30–31: Universal Images Group/SuperStock; 31tl: Wave Royalty Free/age fotostock; 31tc: Trans-World Photos/SuperStock; 31tr: Victor Englebert/Photo Researchers, Inc.; 31br: Wave Royalty Free/Alamy; 32tl: John Mitchell/Photo Researchers, Inc.; 32tr: Alex Wild; 32b, 33tl, 33tc: Thomas Marent; 33r: Patrick Landmann/Photo Researchers, Inc.; 34–35: Thomas Marent; 36tl: TommL/iStockphoto; 36tr: Dr. Morley Read/Shutterstock; 36cl: shane partridge/iStockphoto; 36cml: Peter Wollinga/Dreamstime; 36cmr: Magdalena Bujak/Shutterstock; 36cr: kochanowski/Shutterstock; 36b: Charles McRae/Visuals Unlimited, Inc.; 37: Pete Oxford/Nature Picture Library; 38l: Cezary Wojtkowski/age fotostock; 38–39: Chris Gallagher/Photo Researchers, Inc.; 38c, 38tr: Thomas Marent; 38bc: iStockphoto/Thinkstock; 38br: Eric Isselée/Shutterstock; 39tr: Alex Wild; 39bl: Minden Pictures/SuperStock; 39bcl, 39bcr, 39br, 40–41: Thomas Marent; 42–43: Bruce Davidson/NPL/Minden Pictures; 42tl: Planetary Visions Ltd.; 43t: iStockphoto/Thinkstock; 43ct: Guenter Guni/iStockphoto; 43cm: Nico Smit/iStockphoto; 43cb: Krzysztof Wiktor/Fotolia; 43cb (background): Thomas Marent; 43b: Jordana Meilleur/iStockphoto; 44bl: Minden Pictures/Masterfile; 44tr: Tony Camacho/Photo Researchers, Inc; 44–45: Thomas Marent; 45tl: Steve Cukrov/Shutterstock; 45tc, 45tr: Minden Pictures/Masterfile; 45br: Sergey Uryadnikov/Alamy; 46–47 (background): Rob Broek/iStockphoto; 46–47 (tree stumps): Eddisonphotos/iStockphoto; 46l: Asia Images Group Pte Ltd/Alamy; 46cl, 46cr: iStockphoto/Thinkstock; 46r: Martin Harvey/Corbis; 47l: iStockphoto/Thinkstock; 47cl: Hemera/Thinkstock; 47cr: Margaret Stephenson/Shutterstock; 47r: Eric Isselée/iStockphoto; 48–49: Nick Garbutt/SteveBloom.com; 48tl: Planetary Visions Ltd.; 49t: Frank Vassen/Wikimedia Commons; 49ct: Jameson Weston/Shutterstock; 49cb: Anthony Aneese Totah Jr/Dreamstime; 49b: Henkbentlage/Dreamstime; 50–51: Dr. Matjaž Kuntner; 51tr: GalliasM/Wikimedia Commons; 52 (hammerheaded flying fox): Merlin Tuttle/BCI/Photo Researchers, Inc.; 52 (Goliath bird-eating spider): Amwu/Dreamstime; 52 (flatid leaf bugs): Thomas Marent; 52 (rhinoceros beetle): Empire331/Dreamstime; 52 (hairy caterpillar): Thomas Marent; 52 (Wilson's bird of paradise): Doug Janson/Wikimedia Commons; 52 (margined-winged stick insect): andrewburgess/Fotolia; 52 (Hercules beetle): Cosmin Manci/Dreamstime; 52 (leaf mimic katydid): iStockphoto/Thinkstock; 52 (fungi): Thomas Marent; 52 (red-eyed tree frog): 1stGallery/Shutterstock; 52 (Brazilian armadillo): Minden Pictures/SuperStock; 52 (orchid mantis): Eric Isselée/Fotolia; 52 (tarsier): Marcus Lindström/iStockphoto; 53 (lantern fly): Thomas Marent; 53 (thorn bugs): Jeffrey Lepore/Photo Researchers, Inc.; 53 (Fleischmann's glass frog, dead leaf grasshopper): Thomas Marent; 53 (southern cassowary): Stefanie Dollase-Berger/Shutterstock; 53 (green vine snake): Matthew Cole/Shutterstock; 53 (hissing cockroaches): Chichinkin/Shutterstock; 53 (spiny devil katydid): Morley Read/iStockphoto; 53 (giant blue earthworm): Fletcher & Baylis/Photo Researchers, Inc.; 53 (peanut-head bug): Ismael Montero Verdu/iStockphoto; 53 (great hornbill): Wizreist/Dreamstime; 53 (chameleon): Thomas Marent; 53 (leaf insect): Isselee/Dreamstime; 53 (king vulture): Eric Isselée/Fotolia; 54–55: BirDiGoL/Shutterstock; 54tl: Planetary Visions Ltd.; 55t: Aleksandrs Jemeljanovs/Dreamstime; 55ct: Sergey Uryadnikov/Dreamstime; 55cb: Fletcher & Baylis/Photo Researchers, Inc.; 55b: Iorboaz/Dreamstime; 56–57: Steve Winter/National Geographic Stock; 56tr: Stephen Dalton/Photo Researchers, Inc.; 56 (bats): Dean Bertoncelj/Dreamstime; 56bl: lightpoet/Shutterstock; 57tl: Stéphane Bidouze/iStockphoto; 57tr: Steven Puetzer/Getty Images; 57cl: Barry Mansell/SuperStock; 57br: Vitaly Titov/Dreamstime; 58–59: Eye Ubiquitous/Alamy; 58tr: Szefei/Dreamstime; 58bl: Gavriel Jecan/age fotostock; 59tl, 59tc: Eric Baccega/NPL/Minden Pictures; 59tr: George Steinmetz/National Geographic Stock; 60–61, 62–63t: Thomas Marent; 62cl: iStockphoto/Thinkstock; 62bl: Ralf Hettler/iStockphoto; 62bc: David Parsons/iStockphoto; 62br: Cristian Baitg/iStockphoto; 63t: Chris Lorenz/Dreamstime; 63bl: Stockbyte/Thinkstock; 63bcl: Irogova/Dreamstime; 63bcr: Mynametp1/Dreamstime; 63br: Josef Mohyla/iStockphoto; 64tl: Floortje/iStockphoto; 64tr: Ewen Cameron/iStockphoto; 64bl: Nikita Starichenko/Shutterstock; 64br: Aquariagirl1970/Dreamstime; 65tl: sursad/Shutterstock; 65tc: nullplus/iStockphoto; 65tr: Catherine Ursillo/Photo Researchers, Inc.; 65bl: Semen Lixodeev/Shutterstock; 65br: Kati Molin/iStockphoto; 66–67: KoenSuyk/age fotostock; 66cl: Brasil2/iStockphoto; 66cm: Maria Toutoudaki/iStockphoto; 66tr: Ton Koene/age fotostock/SuperStock; 67tl, 67tcl: iStockphoto/Thinkstock; 67tcr: eAlisa/Shutterstock; 67tr: Jupiterimages/Thinkstock; 68–69 (background): Josef Friedhuber/iStockphoto; 68bl: Thomas Marent; 68–69 (gorilla): erwinf/Shutterstock; 69tl: LifesizeImages/iStockphoto; 69tc: Media Bakery; 69tr: Zeliha Vergnes/iStockphoto; 69bc: Thomas Marent; 69br: Hemera/Thinkstock; 70–71 (branch), 70 (rhinoceros hornbill): iStockphoto/Thinkstock; 70 (imperial parrot): Petra Wegner/Alamy; 70 (tapir): Ammit/Dreamstime; 70 (Madagascar serpent eagle): E.R. Degginger/Alamy; 70 (golden dragon fish): 4155878100/Shutterstock; 70 (hyacinth macaw): Isselee/Dreamstime; 70 (great green macaw): Evgeniapp/Dreamstime; 70 (Bali starling): Leung Cho Pan/Dreamstime; 70 (Philippine eagle): Edwin Verin/Dreamstime; 70 (Queen Alexandra's birdwing butterfly): dieKleinert/Alamy; 70 (manatee): 33karen33/iStockphoto; 70 (red-headed vulture): Gvision/Dreamstime; 70 (giant otter): Kevin Schafer/Media Bakery; 71 (black-handed spider monkey): Lunamarina/Dreamstime; 71 (white-cheeked gibbon l): Mitja Mladkovic/Dreamstime; 71 (white-cheeked gibbon r): Andras Deak/Dreamstime; 71 (glasswing butterfly): Alessandro Zocchi/iStockphoto; 71 (rufous hornbill): Petra Wegner/Alamy; 71 (poison dart frog): Eric Isselée/iStockphoto; 71 (red-crowned Amazon parrot): Anthony Mercieca/Photo Researchers, Inc.; 71 (golden mantella frog): Eric Isselée/Fotolia; 71 (yellow-crested cockatoo): Isselee/Dreamstime; 71 (gorilla): Iexan/Fotolia; 71 (Spix's macaw): Claus Meyer/Getty Images; 71 (katydid): Thomas Marent; 71 (postman butterfly): John Pitcher/iStockphoto; 71 (chimpanzee): Judy Tejero/Fotolia; 71 (treehopper): Patrick Landmann/Photo Researchers, Inc.; 71 (black-and-white ruffed lemur): Lukas Blazek/Dreamstime; 71 (Sumatran tiger): Eric Isselée/Shutterstock; 71 (golden-headed lion tamarin): Isselee/Dreamstime; 71 (electric blue gecko): Mgkuijpers/Dreamstime; 72–73 (background): Thomas Marent; 72 (butterfly): Jeff Grabert/Dreamstime; 72 (bamboo): iStockphoto/Thinkstock; 72 (scorpion), 73 (leaf): Thomas Marent; 73 (vine): Stephane Bidouze/Shutterstock; 73 (ants): Thomas Marent; 73 (campfire): Jupiterimage/Thinkstock; 73 (toucan): Eduardo Mariano Rivero/iStockphoto; 74tr, 74bl: Rainforest Rescue International; 74–75 (leeches): szefei/Shutterstock; 75br: Hornbil Images/Alamy; 76–77: Hemera/Thinkstock; 78: Kheng Ho Toh/Dreamstime; 79: Wisnu Haryo Yudhanto/Dreamstime.

Cover

Background: Antonio Jorge Nunes/Shutterstock. Front cover: (tl) Jeff Grabert/Dreamstime; (c) Thomas Marent; (bl) Nick Garbutt/Nature Picture Library; (br) Lunamarina/Dreamstime. Back cover: (tr) fivespots/Shutterstock; (computer monitor) Manaemedia/Dreamstime.